Washington

Public Safety Employees

Members Handbook

Second Edition

Cline and Associates
2003 Western Avenue North, Suite 550
Seattle, Washington 98121

ISBN-13: 978-0692280133

ISBN-10: 0692280138

Editor: Darrah Hinton
Cover Design: Steve Pillitu

Acknowledgement

First, I have to credit my clients who remind me not only of the need for this information, but also kept producing interesting problems, giving me seemingly endless materials with which to write. This book is dedicated to you. I find your public service to be inspiring, and it motivates me to continue serving you every day, with all the effort I can muster.

I have to thank those who assisted in the First Edition upon which this Second Edition was built: Paulette Pettis, Juliet Jones, and Jennifer Campbell. With the help of Cline and Associates Officer Manager, Darrah Hinton, we were able to construct a Second Edition that is hopefully even better and more readable than the First. Darrah always seems especially effective, both here and in our Firm's Newsletter, of locating the best clip art to bring a point of law to life.

I also wanted to credit our Firm's graphic designer (and my grade school and high school classmate), Steve Pillitu. When you want something done reliably, it's often good to go back to old friends. Steve guided us through the transition of this booklet from its previous hard copy format, into an E-Book format that, we hope, allows a wider and more effective dissemination of this important information.

We printed 10,000 copies of the First Edition and managed to distribute those. With new technology, it is my hope that this edition achieves more cost-effective and widespread circulation.

Table of Contents

"The petitioner may have a constitutional right to talk politics, but he has no constitutional right to be a policeman. There are few employments for hire in which the servant does not agree to suspend its constitutional right to free speech, as well as the vitalness, by the implied term of his contract. The servant cannot complain, as he takes the employment on the terms which are offered him..."

Oliver Wendell Holmes, *McAuliffe v. New Bedford,* 115 Mass. 216, 220, 29 N.E. 517, at 517-18 (1902).

"We conclude that policemen, like teachers and lawyers, are not relegated to a watered-down version of constitutional rights. There are rights of constitutional stature, whose exercise the state may not condition by the exaction of a price."

Garrity v. New Jersey, 385 U.S. 493, 499 (1967).

Introduction

You also have Legal Rights

This booklet is dedicated to you, the public safety employees in the State of Washington, who protect and serve the citizens in this state. You are called upon to respect the legal rights of these citizens. When you don't comply with the legal rules, discipline, criminal charges, lawsuits and sometimes loss of career will follow.

The "*Miranda* Rights" are the most well-known example of such rights. The *Miranda* decision requires law enforcement officers to begin suspect interrogation with an affirmative advisement: "You have the right to remain silent; you have a right to an attorney...." These rights are so well-known to the public at large that the suspects themselves can probably recite their rights without any advisement.

But public safety employees also have legal rights. And in my experience, I'm sad to say, a number of public safety managers remain ignorant about, or indifferent to these rights. At times, they practically act as if they are living in 1902, that time when the "servant" could not "complain as he takes the employment on the terms which are offered to him." Employees are frequently disciplined when they fail to accord citizens their full rights. But in my experience, department managers and supervisors are rarely disciplined for their failure to respect their own employees' rights.

If public employers took their obligation to comply with the law seriously, wouldn't they be disciplining managers and supervisors who violate employees' rights? You would think so, but until that happens, employees—with the help of their representatives—will have to protect them.

And that, in turn, will require knowledge about those rights. It is this important need that this booklet seeks to address.

Jim Cline
Seattle, Washington

I. The Right of Employees to a Fair Discipline Process

Public safety employees have a number of constitutional and statutory rights that ensure that the procedures used to investigate disciplinary charges are fair and proper. In addition, labor agreements require that discipline be imposed only for "just cause."

A. The Right to a Fair and Legal Investigation

1. *Weingarten* Rights: The Right to Union Representation

The "*Weingarten*" rule, originally adopted by the National Labor Relations Board (NLRB) and approved by the United States Supreme Court, has been adopted and applied by the Washington

> **THE OBLIGATION IS UPON THE EMPLOYEE TO REQUEST A UNION REPRESENTATIVE**

State Public Employment Relations Commission (PERC). This rule requires that an employee subject to discipline be permitted, upon request, to have a union representative during a discipline investigation.

There are two key elements to the *Weingarten* right. First, the employee must have a reasonable belief that the meeting could result in disciplinary action. Second, the employee must have explicitly made the request for a union representative.

Right must be Expressly Asserted. The obligation is not upon the employer to advise an employee of their right to a union representative: *It must be expressly requested by the employee.* But the employer may not mislead the employee in a waiver of this right by engaging "subterfuge" about the purpose of the meeting. Once an employee has requested a representative, the employer must either acknowledge that right or discontinue the interview. Once an employee requests representation, the right to representation remains in full effect for any and all subsequent meetings.

Role of Union Representative. The role of a union representative is broad. While the union representative may not fundamentally impede an employer's ability to perform the investigative interview, the union representative's role is *not* limited to that of a quiet observer. The role of a union representative is also to be an active participant at critical junctures. This role includes:

- Making objections to misleading, improper or unlawful questions;
- Asking for clarification of unclear questions;
- Offering additional evidence at an appropriate time in the proceeding;
- Requesting breaks for the employee when necessary.

An employee may also request reasonable intermissions to consult with the union representative.

2. *Garrity* Rights: The Right against Involuntary Incrimination.

The Fifth Amendment of the United States Constitution protects individuals against self-incrimination. The right to be free from self-incrimination includes the right not to be coerced or compelled to give a statement that could be used against you in a criminal matter. You might not think this right to be especially important until you consider the range of Federal and State laws that make civil rights violations, or other misconduct, at least potentially subject to criminal prosecution.

This Fifth Amendment issue requires a balancing, on the one hand, of the public employee's right not to incriminate oneself against, on the other hand, the public employer's right to enforce standards of conduct. The enforcement of such standards necessarily requires that the agency investigate misconduct allegations that may be criminal. This section addresses the approach courts have developed to balance and respect both sets of rights.

Garrity Rule. *Garrity v. New Jersey* is a criminal case concerning the admissibility of compelled statements of police officers. During an internal investigation, the officers were ordered to talk and were told if they did not, they would be fired. When they did speak, they were later charged criminally, and their statements were used in the criminal proceeding.

> **TO BE PROTECTED BY THE GARRITY RULE, A PROPER "ORDER" MUST BE ISSUED.**

The officers were convicted in a criminal proceeding, and they appealed their convictions all the way to the United States Supreme Court. The Court overturned their convictions, holding that the statements were inadmissible in the criminal proceeding because they were coerced. The Court explained:

> The choice given petitioners was either to forfeit their jobs or to incriminate themselves. The option to lose their means of livelihood or to pay the penalty of self-incrimination is the antithesis of free choice to speak out or remain silent.

Importance of Order. For a public safety employee to be protected by the *Garrity* rule, a proper "order" must be issued. A statement that is voluntarily provided is *not* given under the protection of *Garrity* and *may be used in the criminal proceeding.*

Sometimes questions arise as to whether an actual "order" has been given. It is *always* important to clarify that an actual order is being given. Although courts have sometimes allowed *Garrity* protection to employees when they had a reasonable belief that they were providing a statement under an order, the case law in this area is not clearly defined, and a better practice is to ensure that a clear order has been issued.

I find this ambiguous "order" problem is often an issue in paramilitary organizations like police departments because the idea of following an implied order is ingrained through training and police culture. When facing an expectation to submit a statement in critical circumstances, such as lethal force situations (discussed below), it is important to stop and ask if you are *actually* being ordered to provide a statement.

On occasion, an employer will provide *both* a *Miranda* warning and a *Garrity* warning *at the same time*! If this is done, the union representative should object. And the employee should then refuse further questions *until the employer puts in writing exactly what act the employee is being compelled to do.*

Keep in mind that there are a number of subtle contexts in which criminal issues may arise during an internal investigation. For public safety employees, as we suggested above, the scope of what *could* be "criminal" does not just extend to the everyday "crimes." Criminal charges could be brought against public safety employees, for example, for alleged violations of federal civil rights laws or even for misfeasance or nonfeasance in the discharge of a public office.

3. Privacy Rights: The Right to Lawful Investigative Techniques

It is a paramount principle of "just cause" (to be discussed in greater detail later) that investigations be both thorough *and* fair. But those investigations must also be lawful. Here are some typical issues that may occur during investigations in which the lawfulness of the investigative tactics could be at issue:

Polygraphs: RCW 49.44.120 states it is unlawful for an employer to require "directly or indirectly" that an employee be subjected to a polygraph. (Washington state law does not prohibit an employer from requesting a polygraph and if you are asked to submit to a polygraph you should immediately consult with your union and, preferably, your union attorney.)

Work Area and Locker Searches: In 1987, the Supreme Court addressed the issue of a public employer searching the work area of an employee and the principles established there still mostly define this area of law. In this decision, *O'Conner v. Ortega*, the Court established the following principles:

1. That employees *may* have a "reasonable expectation of privacy" in their office space, but that a determination needs to be made on a case-by-case basis, because the actual existence of such a "reasonable expectation" depends on the totality of circumstances and the work environment;

2. Where the employer is investigating a matter which is work related, the constitutional requirement for a warrant in inapplicable;

3. While waiving the warrant requirement for workplace searches, the Court still restrains the employer, holding it to a "reasonable suspicion" standard.

There is still some uncertainty after *Ortega* under what conditions lockers may be searched. Departments sometimes have issued guidelines indicating that there is no reasonable expectation to privacy in a locker.

The theory apparently is that this leaves it open to a warrantless search, but that still remains much in doubt. Clearly where the employer has not stated that the lockers are the property of the employer and may be searched, there likely is a reasonable expectation of privacy.

Body Searches: Courts have recognized that strip searches and body searches are extremely intrusive, and public employees have a constitutional right in connection with such searches. The tests for determining whether such a search in the workplace is valid has generally been held to be the "reasonable suspicion" standard.

Home Searches: The Ninth Circuit has ruled that it is a violation of the Fourth Amendment for a police department to conduct a warrantless search on a police officer's home simply because the investigation is part of an internal affairs investigation. The Ninth Circuit reinstated an officer who refused to comply with an unlawful order that he consent to a search of his home. The Employer's broad power to conduct workplace searches stops at the abode.

Drug Tests: The United States Supreme Court has issued a pair of opinions regarding the public employer's right to perform drug tests on its employees. But these cases only partially clarified when employees can be subject to drug testing. The holdings of these two cases are:

1. A federal regulation mandating drug testing without any reasonable suspicion of railroad employees involved in an accident is justified in the light of the safety issues at stake.

2. The Customs Department is allowed to undertake drug testing of applicants without reasonable suspicion when the applicants are applying for positions involving either drug interdiction or the carrying of a weapon.

Recently, courts have upheld random drug testing of corrections officers while requiring individualized reasonable suspicion of police officers. Some courts have shown a greater willingness to allow random testing for those police officers directly involved in narcotics investigations. Whether random testing can be applied to other law enforcement officers is an unresolved question. Other state courts have allowed the application of random testing for officers, but Washington State has yet to address it. For other less safety sensitive public safety positions, it also remains unresolved, yet unlikely that random testing would be permitted. (At times, random testing is applied for employees with documented substance abuse issues, but that is done through a three way agreement involving the employer, the union and the individual employee.)

4. *Loudermill* Rights: The Right to Pre-disciplinary Due Process

Courts have held that, under the United States Constitution, public employees with "tenure" have a property right in their jobs and are entitled to due process. Due process may be required when employee "liberty" interests are at stake.

> **DUE PROCESS REQUIRES THE EMPLOYEE RECEIVE NOTICE OF THE CHARGES, AN EXPLANATION OF THE EVIDENCE, AND AN OPPORTUNITY TO PRESENT THE EMPLOYEE'S SIDE OF THE STORY.**

Property Rights. In a procedural due process case, the court applies a two-step constitutional rights analysis. First, the court asks whether a "property interest" exists that would entitle the individual to due process. Second, *if* a property interest exists, *then* the court will apply a balancing test to determine what process is due.

In *Board of Education v. Loudermill,* the U.S.

Supreme Court applied these two tests to conclude that public employees with tenure were entitled to a pre-termination hearing *before* being fired. If the government agency has established that an employee will be discharged only for cause, that employee would be considered to have a property interest in continued employment. Not only does the Constitution require an information pre-termination hearing, it generally requires a full post-discharge evidentiary hearing.

Collective Bargaining Agreement (CBA) language or civil service rules that prohibit the discipline without cause have been ruled sufficient to create a protected property interest. (Even probationary employees may have a right to due process if their "liberty interest" is affected by a discharge which damages their reputation.)

"Property rights" extend to more than just whether an employee keeps their job, but almost to any loss of wages. For example, courts have almost uniformly ruled that short-term suspensions are subject to the *Loudermill* requirement. Courts are divided about whether transfers out of a special assignment invoke the due process requirements but if there is a loss of pay premium, it likely is subject to the requirements. Demotions from a civil service position or other higher paid "classifications" almost certainly do invoke the due process requirements. Courts have even held that removal from a civil service list invokes *Loudermill* rights.

The Process which is "Due." *Loudermill* due process requires a "full evidentiary hearing" eventually but not prior to termination. Prior to termination, only an informal conference is required. But before that informal hearing the employee has a right receive notice of the charges, an explanation of the evidence, and an opportunity to present their side of the story.

CBA "Bill of Rights." Public safety employee contracts, especially police contracts, frequently include a "Bill of Rights." These Bill of Rights frequently spells out even more specific procedural requirements an employer must fulfill before, during, and after the disciplinary investigative process. Because some aspects of these pre-discipline rights are subject to changing court rulings and competing interpretations, a written Bill of Rights may be useful for all concerned. Clear guidelines not only protect the rights of employees, they also provide clear guidance for employers and supervisors to follow.

B. Right of Employees to be Disciplined Only for Just Cause: 19 Tests

In Washington, there is a dual discipline appeal system: civil service and arbitration under a CBA. Almost all public safety employees in Washington are covered under civil service. But civil service generally only provides limited protection: The standards typically applied by most civil service commissions in discipline appeals, are extremely deferential to the employer.

So, if you are disciplined or discharged, you want to look first to your CBA and grievance procedure, not civil service. Arbitrators are labor relations professionals who are truly "neutral" in that both parties have had a hand in selecting them. Furthermore, arbitrators apply a broader notion of "just cause." If, for some reason, you lack the support of your union and cannot pursue a grievance to arbitration under your CBA, civil service appeals may be all that you have, but experience indicates such appeals are often doomed at the start.

As said, arbitrators apply a broader idea of what is required under "just cause." The factors that make up "just cause" are not technically or legally complex. They are basically common sense. The overarching requirement of just cause is that people be treated with due process and fundamental fairness. A review of published Arbitration decisions shows that arbitrators tend to apply up to 19 tests for just cause:

1. **Notice of Charges:** Process requires notice of the charges to the employee. Employees need to know why they are being disciplined and, as well, unions need to understand the charges so that they can prepare a defense at the hearing. Notice must be precise both as to the nature of the charge and the nature of the rule charged.

2. **Notice of Rule:** An employer must establish that the employee either knew or *should have known* about the existence of the rule. A rule need *not* be in writing (although the lack of writing may cause a challenge to the actual existence of the rule). Generally, the employees simply need some type of notice that there is a rule.

   There is one exception to the formal notice requirement. This occurs when the arbitrator finds that the employee was put on "constructive" notice. This type of notice extends to conduct that is so egregious that it simply is not done by responsible employees, *even though* not specifically prohibited in the past. There are a limited number of examples of this type of conduct such for general employees as stealing, intoxication at work, and fighting but for public safety employees the list is longer and it reflects all the training and experience that leads someone to simply know not to do something.

3. **Notices to the penalty:** Employees have a right, not only to notice of the rule, but also the *expected penalty* for violating the rule. This type of notice is especially important when the employer attempts to impose a more severe penalty on a rule violation, than has been imposed in the past. Notice to the penalty is especially important when termination is at issue.

4. **Consistency in Rule Enforcement:** It is not

enough simply to publish a rule and not enforce it. Sporadic enforcement of a rule may cause an arbitrator to conclude that employees have not truly been put on notice that not following a rule is wrong.

5. ***Reasonableness of a Rule:*** Arbitrators will only enforce "reasonable" rules. For a rule to be reasonable, there must be some rational relationship to the employer's operations.

6. ***Thorough and Fair Investigation:*** Arbitrators have consistently held that employers who seek to discipline employees must first obtain as much information as reasonably possible, including statements from all key witnesses, and *especially* a statement from the employee. Discipline decisions are often overturned by the failure of the employer to investigate cases thoroughly before imposing discipline. A demonstrated bias by the investigator can also lead to discipline being set aside.

7. ***Legal and Contractual Due Process:*** The just cause standard involves many "due process" requirements which usually at least means some type of "fundamental fairness" in the entire process. There are a number of additional due process requirements public employers owe their employees. These include the prediscipline procedure rights discussed above: *Weingarten*, *Loudermill*, and, where written into the CBA, the Bill of Rights. Violations of these constitutional, statutory or contractual rights frequently are the basis for setting aside discipline that might otherwise be supported by the evidence.

8. ***Lawful Evidence Gathering:*** Investigative procedure followed by the employer must not only be thorough and fair, it must also be lawful. An employer's reliance on unlawful polygraphs or unconstitutional searches will usually cause the

discipline to be overturned.

9. ***Employee Violation of a Rule:*** Undoubtedly, this is the *most important* of all of the tests: *If the employee did not do the act that is alleged, no discipline should occur.*

10. **Proportionality:** While no two discipline cases are the same, arbitrators expect some *rough* equality in the discipline of employees committing similar infractions. The difficulty in comparing different discipline is that often factors other than the nature of the violation itself warrant the discipline imposed. For example, factors such as the employees' length and quality of service of the employees involved, their record of discipline, and other mitigating factors, all are reasonably considered by the employer and these factors may legitimately cause them to treat employees differently for what seems to be the same exact offense

11. **Progressive Discipline:** One of the primary reasons discipline is overturned by arbitrators is *the failure of employers to follow standards of progressive discipline.* Progressive discipline involves discipline in escalating severity with the purpose of providing notice and opportunity for correction. The central idea of "progressive discipline" is that the discipline should be "corrective," not punitive. Arbitrators, though, will excuse employers from the progressive discipline requirement in a narrow set of offenses known as "capital offenses" — those offenses which clearly rupture the employer-employee relationship and, because of that, returning the employee to work is not feasible.

12. ***Employer Interest in the Rule:*** The nature of the employer's interest in the enforcement of the rule has a strong bearing on the overall reasonableness of the discipline. Violations of less significant rules may warrant less significant discipline, and

violation of more significant rules may warrant more significant discipline. This factor has to be assessed in the context and nature of the workplace. For law enforcement, for example, the obligation for officers to follow the law themselves is so important that an officer that commits crimes even of a misdemeanor nature could be subject to significant discipline.

13. ***Reasonableness of the Penalty:*** This test measures the *overall* balancing of the competing factors. When a violation is more severe in nature, such as a capital offense, immediate termination may be warranted despite lengthy service and a clean discipline record. On the other hand, an employee with a brief period of service marked by frequent disciplinary infractions can be terminated for less significant rule violation. The general rule, though, is that except in a case of a very serious offense, just cause requires that employers invoke the steps of progressive discipline before imposing the ultimate penalty of termination.

14. ***Mitigating Factors:*** There is a variety of mitigating factors that might arise in any situation and the employer must consider these before imposing the discipline. For example, arbitrators might set aside discipline where the management is at fault in some respect or the employee's conduct can be explained by some personal problem. Mitigating factors are not necessarily a guaranteed defense, but an equitable factor that arbitrators will consider. It is the overall circumstances that will be weighed and balanced and mitigating factors are one of those circumstances.

15. ***Double Jeopardy:*** Employers can only discipline an employee *once* for the same offense. For example, if a supervisor issues a reprimand, but later want to impose a more severe penalty, most arbitrators will find the supervisors' action

binding on the employer — even if the higher level management had had no input.

16. **Fault of the Employer:** If the employer is at fault or if it has not provided the proper training or resources, or had provoked the employee, arbitrators will often set the discipline aside.

17. **Employer's Motivation and Reasoning Process:** If an employer is unable to explain clearly what legitimate rational supports the discipline, or if the employer otherwise relies on inadmissible or unsubstantiated evidence, arbitrators often overturn the discipline. Often these sources of problems in the employer's case are only discovered during the course of the arbitration hearing.

18. **Obligation of Accommodation:** Arbitrators generally recognize that "just cause" requires employers to comply with all statutes, including discrimination statutes. Employers are especially held to this requirement where they have agreed to a "nondiscrimination" clause in the CBA. For example, when an employee has a medical disability that could contribute to the rule violation alleged, an arbitrator *may* set the discipline aside. This is not a guaranteed defense, of course, because, as will be discussed below, the employer is only required to "reasonably" accommodate such disabilities.

19. **Violation of Employee Civil Rights:** Public safety employees have a number of statutory and constitutional rights, discussed below, such as the right to free speech or the right to privacy. Disciplinary actions which violate these rights can be expected to be overturned by an arbitrator.

16 Tips for Employees Facing Discipline

1. If you are unsure whether questioning could lead to discipline, always be safe — *ask for your union representative.*

2. Ask, or have your union representative ask, *what* you are being accused of. Ask to be provided a description of the complaint.

3. Before the interview, review the complaint and the surrounding circumstances with your union representative. Be candid about all the circumstances with your union representative. The  representative cannot be as helpful when faced with "surprises" during the interview.

4. Obtain an "order" before answering questions. If you volunteer without an order, you lose your *Garrity* protections order.

5. During the interview, listen to the questions carefully. *Only answer the question asked.* Don't guess as to what you think is being asked if it isn't clear. If the question is confusing, ask for clarification.

6. Ask to consult with your union representative at any time during the interview. You have the right to consult privately with your union representative upon request.

7. Be truthful. Untruthfulness may be grounds for discharge even if the underlying misconduct is not. If you made a misstatement, consult with your union representative about it and clarify your answer.

8. Remain *calm* throughout the interview. The investigation may be stressful and something

that you have never faced before, but concentrate on keeping your emotions in check. *Anger can be turned against you during an interrogation.*

9. If you failed to ask for a union representative before the interview but now find out the interview has developed to the point where you now want a representative, *ask for one.* You can ask for a representative at any time during the interview *even if* you didn't ask for one before.

10. If there are any follow-up interviews, be sure the union representative is aware of them. The employer is obligated to tell the union representative of the follow-up interview, but you should verify that they did.

11. Do not consent to *any* "off the record" questions. Be sure the interview is recorded. Discrepancies in unrecorded interviews *never* work to the advantage of the employee. If there is a dispute over what was said and you are the accused, almost always the investigator's "interpretation" of what you said is more likely to be adopted.

12. If the employer requests a polygraph, *decline.* Participation in such a polygraph is usually more likely to hurt than help. It may depend on the context but at the early stages of the investigation you simply do not know the complete context yet. In any event, participation in a polygraph should be done only after consultation with the union representative *and* union counsel.

13. If you receive a "pre-disciplinary" hearing "notice," *be sure* your union representative is aware of it and can attend. Prepare for the hearing with your representative.

14. Likewise, do not consent to any search of your property or locker without first

consulting with your representative.

15. If the department disciplines you, you have the right to appeal. *Consult with your union representative immediately.* Do not file a civil service appeal without first checking with your representative — you may be giving up your right to file a grievance because most CBAs contain what is called an "election of remedies" clause. Comply with all instructions for filing grievances. *An untimely appeal will be a lost appeal.*

16. If you want to pursue a grievance, cooperate fully with your union representative. The union will need as much information as possible to assess the grievance.

II. The Rights of Injured and Disabled Public Safety Employees

This section discusses state and federal disability discrimination laws, pregnancy discrimination laws, and the Family Medical Leave Act (FMLA). These laws are complex, often interrelated among themselves and also interrelated with the requirements of your CBA.

A. State and Federal Disability Discrimination Laws

Employees are protected by a number of disability laws — both state and federal. Generally, these laws require employers to attempt to accommodate employees with medical conditions. But these laws require only "reasonable" accommodations and do *not* require employers to retain employees who are unable to perform the "essential" requirements of the job.

Light Duty/Job Restructuring. Both the state and federal law are fairly clear that there is no obligation to create "permanent" light duty programs. It should be noted, though, that where there is a light duty program in place, this is a mandatory subject of bargaining. Courts have ruled that if public safety employees cannot perform the "essential functions" of the job — which often includes using force — the employer does *not* have an obligation to restructure the position.

Rotating Shift Issues. Often, individuals have a disability which impairs their ability to work around-the-clock, or at least in frequently rotating shifts. Diabetes is an example of a disability that impedes some individual's ability to rotate through the shifts because of the health implications of such schedule changes. Whether an individual can be accommodated in this manner largely depends on the nature of the department. If this accommodation would substantially adversely affect other employees, it is likely that a court will find that this is not a reasonable accommodation. If there are a number of employees in the same classification and the employee can easily be rescheduled, the court would likely find that it is an accommodation that should be made.

Mental Health. There is an obligation to accommodate people with mental health issues, if the accommodation would still allow them to perform the essential functions of the job. An employee with such issues should come forward as needed to get help to make the necessary work adjustments. With mental disabilities in particular, though, courts have imposed duties on employers to recognize the signs in advance and be proactive and fully engaged in assessing the situation.

Alcoholism. There has been considerable conflict in court decisions between the American with Disabilities Act (ADA), the Rehabilitation Act, and state disability law concerning whether and how alcoholism can be accommodated. The Rehabilitation Act and state law seem to require *some degree* of accommodation *even when the alcoholism produces on-the-job impacts.* The ADA, though, has been primarily interpreted *not* to require  accommodation of alcoholism to the extent employee conduct involves a violation of a work rule. The extent of "protection" these laws offer concerning alcoholism depends very much on context.

B. Pregnancy Discrimination

Pregnant employees have *some protection* under the Pregnancy Discrimination Act (PDA) and the FMLA, but *little* under the ADA. Under the ADA, pregnancy is *not* considered a "disability." The only exception is pregnancy-related medical complications.

The PDA broadly prohibits discrimination by employers against pregnant employees *because of* their pregnancy, childbirth, or related medical conditions. The PDA requires that pregnant employees be treated the same for employment-related purposes as other persons not pregnant, when otherwise similar in their ability, or inability to work. In other words, if an employer accommodates an individual with medical limitations and creates either a short or long-term disability policy, pregnant employees must have at least the same rights. For purposes of the PDA, pregnancy must be treated at least as favorably as a disability under employer disability policies.

Some have argued that the PDA also grants employees the right to request an accommodation in order to protect their unborn child. These claims have not been successful. Individuals in this situation, instead, will have to look to other rights that one may have under the CBA or the Family Medical Leave Act

(FMLA), which we turn to next.

C. The Right to Family Leave

The FMLA offers additional protections to pregnant employees. *But it also offers protections for other individuals who are injured or disabled.* In fact, it protects *nearly all public safety employees* who can reasonably be anticipated to face some family crisis requiring their absence from work at some point in their careers. The FMLA is intended to balance the interests of employees and their family lives against the interests of the employer to maintain a productive work force.

Under the FMLA, an employee is allowed up to 12 weeks of family leave in any 12-month period. This leave includes care of a newborn child, a newly-adopted child or care of a family member — child, spouse or parent with a "serious health condition." It also permits leave for the employee's own serious health condition.

The employer must allow employees to use all their paid leave banks. When the leave banks are exhausted, the employee then must be allowed to go out on unpaid leave. FMLA leaves must be accompanied with a continuation of the employer's paid health benefits as defined in the CBA.

A common pitfall for employers relates to the duration of the leave. The law permits the employer to count paid leave used when an individual is medically unable to work towards the 12-week FMLA period. But in order to do so, the employer must first give notice to the employee that their 12 weeks has begun to run. When the employer has failed to provide such FMLA notice, the 12 weeks will not begin running until it does so.

Exhaustion of both paid leave and FMLA time does *not* automatically mean the employee can then be discharged. There is a widespread myth to this effect, but it is exactly that — *a myth.* When the leave banks are exhausted, and FMLA period has expired, *if the employee continues to suffer from medical conditions, there may still be an obligation to retain the employee.* The protections of state and federal disability law still apply, and these laws often require the employer to allow, as a "reasonable accommodation," leave up to a year or longer.

III. The Rights of Officers Involved in a Use of Force Incident

Statistics from studies regarding officer-involved shootings reveal some important statistics:

70% of law enforcement officers involved in the use of deadly force will leave police work within 7 years;

- Less than 1% of officer-involved shootings involve criminal culpability;

- The decision to shoot is usually made within 3 seconds;

- 83% of officers involved suffer from time distortion;

- 55% of officers suffer from visual distortion.

All the legal rights of officers that apply during discipline investigations also apply during post-shooting investigations. But there are some particular

> **ALL THE LEGAL RIGHTS THAT APPLY DURING DISCIPLINARY INVESTIGATIONS ALSO APPLY DURING POST-SHOOTING INVESTIGATIONS.**

issues with officer-involved shootings that are likely to arise in connection with these legal rights.

Weingarten Rights. Clearly, *Weingarten* rights fully

apply in a use of force reporting situation. It is prudent to assume that *any* investigation regarding an officer-involved shooting *could* lead to discipline, although in practice, discipline generally does not result.

Any time a law enforcement officer uses lethal force, it has the potential to be criminal in nature. The only difference between criminal homicide and justifiable homicide is that, in the latter, the elements of justification are met. It certainly would be prudent for any law enforcement employee before giving a statement regarding one's use of lethal force to review that statement with an attorney to determine if the elements of justification are met.

One of the difficulties that arises in connection with *Weingarten* is that it does not require the employer to wait for any one particular individual, including the union attorney to be made available. Therefore, absent an agreement to the contrary, the employer could order the employee to give an immediate statement while providing the officer only a limited period of time to arrange for a union representative to be present.

Garrity Rights. Any officer involved in a use of force situation may invoke their constitutional rights under the Fifth Amendment and *Miranda*. When an employer does not give a *Garrity* order, any statement provided by an officer is considered voluntary, and the department, a prosecutor, and the courts may make unlimited use of it.

On the other hand, if the department does not give a *Garrity* order, the officer is in no way required to give a statement *and is free to remain silent.* As discussed earlier, care should be given to determine that an actual *Garrity* order has been issued. A simple "request" by the employer for a statement does *not* constitute a *Garrity* order.

Often, departments will be reluctant to issue a specific *Garrity* order. Chiefs and sheriffs are often urged by prosecutors to avoid giving a *Garrity* order, apparently so the prosecutor's ability later to bring a criminal charge against the officer is not impeded. It is unfortunate that *Garrity* orders are not more forthcoming. It is also unfortunate the degree of manipulation which often follows an officer's refusal to provide a statement without a *Garrity* order. Sometimes it is more or less suggested that

> **WHEN THE EMPLOYER DOES NOT GIVE A GARRITY ORDER, ANY STATEMENT PROVIDED BY AN OFFICER IS CONSIDERED VOLUNTARY AND THE DEPARTMENT, A PROSECUTOR, AND THE COURTS MAY MAKE UNLIMITED USE OF IT.**

the officer should give a statement anyway, with the unfortunate implication that if there is nothing to hide there is no reason not to give a statement.

Often, the pressure at the time and circumstance, including the pressure to appear not to be hiding anything, leads a number of officers to waive their Fifth Amendment rights and provide a statement. These officers should understand that when they do so, unlimited use may be made of these statements. There are different opinions on the importance of asserting *Garrity* rights but my view has been there generally is little to be gained by waiving *Garrity* rights especially in the days and weeks following the incident.

One possible way to circumvent the failure of a chief to give an explicit verbal order is the policies and procedures manual. Often these contain a specific mandate that officers make a report. The case law *arguably* provides some protection *if a statement is given in response to such a written rule. But there is conflict in the case law about this point.* If an officer is going to give a statement anyway, but wants to invoke *Garrity* rights, and the agency has not yet given a clear order, the officer should simply proceed to write a statement and begin the statement with a brief introduction such as: "This is an involuntary statement provided pursuant to the department procedural manual...." Such a statement is not a 100% guarantee of *Garrity* protection, but it will likely hold up if challenged.

Washington law recognizes the following legal privileges (and *only* these privileges) relevant to an officer involved in a use of force situation.

- Spouse
- Attorney
- Psychologist/Psychotherapist
- Priest or Clergy
- Peer Support Counselor

Spousal Privilege. The spousal privilege is virtually absolute, except it does not apply when the statements are made in the presence of a third person. The statutory spousal privilege does *not* apply to unmarried domestic partners.

Attorney Client Privilege. Policies and practices should be developed that clearly put the officer in touch with an attorney who will be the officer's attorney. A handful of departments still have policies requiring officers to talk with the city attorney and/or the prosecutor immediately after the shooting.  Most of these have been withdrawn, but it should be *clear that the prosecutor or city attorney is not the officer's attorney.*

This same issue may occur when the police union arranges for its union counsel to serve as the attorney. There should be an understanding between the union, the attorney, and the officer that, in the context of an officer-involved shooting, the attorney is only representing the employee and not the union. (If disciplinary action later results, obviously the attorney would have a conflict of interest and separate counsel would be necessary to evaluate that discipline case. I have been involved in over 160 lethal force situations as the retained union counsel assisting the employee and a conflict has arisen on only one occasion.)

> **POLICIES AND PRACTICES SHOULD BE DEVELOPED THAT PUT THE OFFICER IN TOUCH WITH AN ATTORNEY WHO WILL BE THE OFFICER'S ATTORNEY.**

Psychologist Privilege. The psychotherapist/psychologist privilege is an important one that allows officers to speak freely regarding their feelings about the incident. Sometimes the department is willing to pay for this psychologist, but care should be taken to ensure that the officer going to a psychologist under this situation has a guarantee of privilege. The employee needs to be assured that this is not simply a fitness for duty examination in which the department is the actual client. Most Washington departments have established such a privilege-preserving protocol, though.

Religious Clergy Privilege. There has been *some confusion* concerning the scope of privileges attached to priests and clergy. Officers should understand that the privilege does not broadly encompass any and all statements they make to personnel employed by church organizations. In *State v. Martin*, the Supreme Court clarified the scope of this privilege. The privilege applies only where:

- The clergy member is ordained;
- The statement is made as part of a "confession in the course of discipline enjoined by the church;"
- Practices or rules of the church to which the clergy or member belongs require that confessions be maintained confidential.

The religious privilege is specifically tailored so that it does *not* encompass any and all types of counseling sessions. An even more important limitation to be aware of is that most likely the department chaplain is *not* covered by the privilege.

Peer Support Counselor Privilege. The most recently recognized statutory privilege, and perhaps one of the most important in this context, is the "peer support group counselor" privilege. But there are a lot of misunderstandings concerning *how* this privilege is acquired. It is important to be aware that the strict terms of the statute must be adhered to. Those terms are defined in the statute. The following conditions must be established for the privilege to attach:

- The individual purporting to be a counselor must receive training to provide emotional or moral support in counseling;
- The counselor must be designated by the departmental chief;
- The designation must occur *prior* to the incident;
- Peer support counselors cannot fulfill that function when the counselor is an "initial responding officer, a witness, or a party to the incident."

In short, it is *not* enough that someone who has been to an officer-involved shooting before simply be considered to be a "peer support" counselor. Such individuals must be specifically appointed by the Chief or Sheriff. A number of departments have failed to take the necessary steps to establish peer support counselors. This is an issue that should be addressed in negotiations ora labor-management meeting.

IV. Rights of Employees to be Represented by a Labor Organization

A. The Right to be Free of Discrimination and Interference for Union Activities

The collective bargaining statute is enforced before the Public Employment Relations Commission (PERC).

PERC makes it an unfair labor practice (ULP) for the employer to "discriminate" against union members based on their union activities *or* to "interfere" in the union's ability to represent its members. It is also an unfair labor practice for a union to discriminate against members. Filing a grievance or participating in union committees are primary examples of protected activities.

"Discrimination" and "interference" are *different forms* of unlawful activity with *different elements*. "Discrimination" involves an *intentional* attempt to retaliate against an employee based on protected activity. "Interference" occurs when the employer, in any way, unduly impedes the ability of the union and its members to operate as an effective labor organization. Sometimes there is overlap between these two charges because an attempt to retaliate against an employee might be discrimination and might also, at the same time, interfere with the union's efforts to represent members.

An interference charge is usually easier to prove because it looks at the management conduct to determine whether it might have a chilling effect on employees without any immediate consideration as to "why" management took that action. In other words, there is no requirement to pro[ve] not controlling in determining by management interfere with it is the ability of a reasonable a statement to be threatening interference.

A STATEMENT BY THE EMPLOYER THAT COULD LEAD AN EMPLOYEE REASONABLY TO BELIEVE THAT THE WORKING CONDITIONS WILL BE ADVERSELY AFFECTED BY THE EMPLOYEE'S PARTICIPATION IN UNION ACTIVITIES WILL FULFILL THE ELEMENTS OF AN INTERFERENCE CHARGE.

Discrimination and interference may occur in a number of situations. The most obvious circumstances include the discipline or discharge of an employee for his union activities. But the prohibition on discrimination extends as well to an employee to protect an employee from being denied a promotion for such activities. A statement by the employer that could lead an employee reasonably to believe that the working conditions will be adversely affected by participation in union activities will fulfill the elements of an interference charge.

Another method of interference is improper employer intermeddling in union activities. It is unlawful for an employer; for example, try to influence internal Guild politics or to spy on the activities of a union. PERC has also found it generally improper to interrogate members regarding what occurs in union meetings.

B. The Right to Bargain Collectively

Labor organizations certified as exclusive bargaining representatives have a special status under Washington law. By statute and case law, they have been assigned the responsibility to represent all the employees on "exclusive" basis in their employment relationship with the employer (whether or not they are even dues paying  members of the union). This union "exclusivity" status includes the sole right to negotiate workplace rules. In other words, employees cannot deal directly or otherwise behind the union's back to work their issues out with the employer.

RCW 41.56.140 provides that a public employer commits a ULP when it refuses to "engage in collective bargaining." The broad scope of the statute requires negotiation "on personnel matters, including wages, hours and working conditions..."

PERC has the primary authority to determine whether a subject falls within the scope of bargaining. The following is a list of highlights of PERC's rulings regarding bargaining subjects most likely to impact public safety employees:

- Wages and wage-related matters are bargainable in nearly all of their forms, including not simply the wage and various wage premiums, but rules concerning out-of-class pay, distribution of overtime, and the schedule for payroll.

- On the other hand, PERC has rejected union efforts to reopen contract negotiations in the light of unanticipated government funds or other union efforts to otherwise compel negotiation over the budget — the budget itself is a management right.

- PERC has taken a very broad view that benefits are bargainable, including the scope of health insurance, health insurance and co-payment premiums, and all types of insurance coverage. PERC has also found other incidental benefits, such as parking, take-home vehicles, and physical fitness programs to be bargainable.

- On the other hand, PERC has determined that the actual identity of the insurance carrier is *not* a mandatory subject of bargaining. The employer may change the carrier, provided the type of benefits remains "substantially similar."

- PERC has taken a broad view that "hours of work"

in *almost all* its forms are bargainable, including the length of the workday, the starting and ending time of the workday, and rest breaks. Proposals to bid for shifts are a mandatory subject of bargaining, as are job sharing programs.

- PERC has also taken a broad view that the subjects of bargaining include almost all forms of leave, including vacation leave, sick leave, and compensatory time. PERC has even ruled that light duty programs are a subject of bargaining.

- The contracting out of bargaining unit work, including the use of reserves or other volunteers is a mandatory subject of bargaining.

- On the other hand, an employer's decision to cease operations or cease providing a service is *not* a subject of bargaining, although it may have to bargain the "impact" of such a decision.

- PERC has found most aspects of discipline and discipline procedures to be bargainable, not only including the right to arbitrate discipline and officer bill of rights, but also rules of conduct.

- PERC has split decisions concerning when various boards constitute a mandatory subject of bargaining, including makeup and operation of citizen review boards.

- Even though discipline and discipline rules are bargainable, the placement of an employee on a performance plan is not.

- Clear numeric activity goals ("quotas") are bargainable, but evaluations are not.

- A substantial change in job duties is likely bargainable, but a job description which merely restates existing duties is not. Also, minor changes in job duties are generally not subject to negotiations.

- Staffing levels and "minimum staffing" are generally not bargainable, except where there is compelling evidence of a safety hazard. On the other hand, an increase in the minimum staffing numbers that directly changes the ability of employees to take leave is negotiable.

- Rules concerning off-duty employment residency and a wide variety of other working conditions concerning employees' private lives will be considered to be a mandatory subject of bargaining. Rules regulating use of tobacco are bargainable, and rules concerning drug testing procedures are bargainable. Rules concerning pre-employment hiring conditions are not bargainable, but application of those rules after the candidate has been retained is bargainable.

- Rules concerning civil service are bargainable but only to the extent that they relate to a wage, hour or working condition. To put in other words, an employer cannot avoid its obligation to bargain by deferring a matter to the civil service commission.

- A wide range of other civil service related issues have also been found bargainable but only to the extent they affect the bargaining unit's conditions of employment. Generally, promotions within the bargaining unit are bargainable, and promotions outside the bargaining unit are not.

- Rules and procedures concerning the

assignment of specialty positions have been found bargainable by PERC.

The notion of a certified collective bargaining representative means that there will be a single agreement which will be *collectively* bargained. Side agreements with individuals are lawful only to the extent the union has acquiesced to the creation of such side agreements. For example, PERC has stricken down a "last chance" agreement concerning a disciplinary issue which was not negotiated with or approved by the union.

Direct negotiations by an employer with employees are generally unlawful. If an officer is meeting with his employer to determine his working conditions and his union representative is not present, the meeting is probably unlawful. *Only the union can negotiate changes in working conditions.*

> **DIRECT NEGOTIATIONS BY AN EMPLOYER ARE GENERALLLY UNLAWFUL. IF YOU ARE MEETING WITH YOUR EMPLOYER TO DETERMINE YOUR WORKING CONDITIONS AND YOUR UNION REPRESENTATIVE IS NOT PRESENT, THE MEETING IS PROBABLY UNLAWFUL.**

The same rules also apply to grievances. If an employee has filed a grievance or the union has filed one on the employee's behalf, it cannot be resolved without the union's knowledge and opportunity for participation. The union has the right to be present at any discussion regarding your grievance. And any grievance settlement cannot conflict with the labor agreement — unless the union agrees with the employer to amend the agreement.

V. The Civil and Constitutional Rights of Public Safety Employees

Public safety personnel who knowingly violate citizens' constitutional rights are subject to discipline. But what happens when an employer violates the constitutional rights of its employees? This section discusses those civil rights issues. The bottom line answer is this: Just as you are obligated to protect the civil rights of the citizens, you also have civil rights that the employer must respect. How those rights operate in a paramilitary workplace is the subject addressed in this discussion.

A. Right to Free Speech

Public employees have a right to free speech. But the difficult question facing a court when dealing with free speech issues is how to balance the free speech rights of public employees against the right of a public employer to operate effectively.

At the very least, it is clear that a public employer may not discharge an employee on the basis that infringes on the employee's constitutionally protected interest in freedom of speech. The determination whether a public employer has properly discharged an employee for engaging in speech requires balancing the interest of the employee, as a citizen — commenting upon matters of public concern — and the interests of the government, as an employer, in promoting the efficiency of the public services it performs through its employees.

The threshold question is whether the employee's speech may be "fairly characterized as constituting speech on a matter of public concern." Only speech that relates to "matters of public concern" is protected under the First Amendment. But even if this speech does address matters of public concern, the employee's interest in making statements must be balanced against the interest of the government, as an employer, in promoting the efficiency of the services it performs through its employees.

In 1968, in *Pickering v. Board of Education*, the Supreme Court firmly established the right of public employees to criticize the policy decisions of a government *even when the government was their employer*. But in 1983, in *Connick v. Meyers,* the Court drew a distinction between employee's speech on matters of public concern which were found to be protected and matters of only personal concern which were found not to be protected.

Since *Connick*, the courts have had to determine whether speech was primarily concerned with a matter of (1) a public concern, or (2) a personal grievance. Moreover, speech affecting a public concern is only protected when it does not "unduly disrupt" the workplace. Speech that occurs as part of everyday work has perplexed the courts in their years since their 1983 *Connick* decision, and they have yet to adopt any clear and consistently followed legal standards for whether work related speech that is critical of the employer is or is not protected.

Certain speech is clearly unprotected: speech which is obscene, profane, defamatory, or involves racial slurs. The speech with the greatest protection under the First Amendment is political speech occurring in a public forum. If a speech pertains to a general issue of public policy, or a public official, it will generally be protected under the First Amendment. Courts have been particularly protective of the right of public employees to speak in public forums outside the workplace.

Many Washington public safety departments have rules purporting to restrict when and how employees may speak. While law enforcement agencies now adopt Lexipol standard and have moved closer to what is required, many rules persist that are unconstitutional because they require prior notice, and sometimes even prior approval, before the employee is permitted to speak on any manner related to department business. These "prior restraint" cases are closely scrutinized by the courts and have difficulty passing constitutional standards.

> **MANY WASHINGTON PUBLIC SAFETY DEPARTMENTS HAVE RULES PURPORTING TO RESTRICT WHEN AND HOW EMPLOYEES MAY SPEAK. MOST OF THESE RULES ARE UNCONSTITUTIONAL.**

Similarly, agencies have adopted "social network" policies that do not uniformly comply with constitutional requirements. The ability of agencies to regulate off-duty speech is limited, and there has been some clear over-reaching in this area as well.

Although there is no clear constitutional right for public employees to engage in partisan political activity, there is a *statutory* right in Washington that gives employees the right to participate in all types of elections.

B. Privacy Rights

1. The Right to Privacy in Medical and Psychological Examinations

Departments have the right to order "fitness for duty" examinations, but they must be able to set forth a clear and sufficient rationale to do so. The ADA *requires* that the department have reasonable grounds to believe that the employee is negatively affecting the operation of the department, i.e., a "business necessity" to compel the examination. Further, *the examination must be job-related.* Often, the threshold is not difficult to meet, but it does require some articulation of exactly *why* the examination is being compelled.

Using a fitness examination as a tool of harassment is unlawful. On the other hand, there are a number of situations in which the employer *will* have a right to compel a medical examination:

- The employee indicates a disability and requests an accommodation;
- It appears that the employee might have a medical limitation which could interfere with the job;
- There is an unexplained performance deficiency;
- The employer (often fire departments) has complied with the EEOC requirements to establish a "periodic physical examination" of the employee — the program must be established under "federal, state or local law" and be consistent with the ADA.

Often, the employer will order the employee to sign a waiver with the doctor, permitting the doctor to freely report information. The legality of these waivers is doubtful because it essentially compels employees to waive their statutory rights under the ADA. Some waivers even seek to keep you from suing the practitioner from negligence in the evaluation process. Our firm has an approved form for such situations, and you should not sign waiver forms without first obtaining review from your union on their validity and legality.

There are also some unresolved questions pertaining to *how much* information department managers are entitled. The ADA is subject to differing interpretations. Perhaps they are only entitled to a conclusion concerning fitness for duty, but possibly the chief is entitled to the entire medical report. At the very least, it is clear that lower ranking managers and supervisors are only entitled to very limited information.

2. Right to Privacy in Personnel Files

Courts have accorded *some* degree of privacy in personnel files. They have also limited the ability of employers to acquire private information that they may not need. when courts have allowed employers to compel employees to complete probing personal questionnaires, courts have also required employers to maintain adequate safeguards to protect this information.

Under Washington law, there are a number of issues concerning the privacy of personnel files that are covered by the Public Disclosure Act. Although the individuals making the request under the Public Disclosure Act are not entitled to broad access to personnel files, the courts have held that there is *no protection* in discipline records which involve sustained acts of misconduct. The law appears to grant no protection to such documents even when they will reveal the identity of the officer.

And in some recent decisions, courts have declined to block disclosure of documents concerned *nonsustained* discipline that, although redacted, providing sufficient clues for most readers to infer the identity of the innocent employee.

3. Right to Maintain Personal Appearance

The courts have consistently rejected claims that uniformed public safety officers have a "liberty" or "privacy" in maintaining grooming appearance and standards of their choice. Courts have uniformly followed *Kelley v. Johnson* holding that the departments have the right to establish hair and grooming standards. These principles apply as well to body art and jewelry. Whether such rules are otherwise subject to the duty to collectively bargain has yet to be determined but there is at least a plausible argument that they are.

.

4. Public Safety Employees' Right to Maintain Private Relationships

Court decisions concerning the right of employees to associate have been given a high degree of protection to public safety employees' right to maintain private relationships, but have allowed restrictions when those relationships have a demonstrative, negative impact on the workplace.

Courts have found the right to marry and the privacy of a marital relationship to be one of the most fundamental constitutional rights. Efforts to extend these rights in cases involving non-marital sexual violations have met with limited and conflicting decisions in various courts. Courts have been quite divided on the question of discipline for employees involved in non-marital sexual relations. Some have held that these are a private matter and employers cannot delve into them. Others have held that these non-marital relationships have no such protection. But some cases are clearly beyond the realm of constitutional protection: The Ninth Circuit has found there is no right to privacy in on-duty sex with a prostitute or off-duty sexual conduct with a 15-year old explorer.

Although courts have almost uniformly upheld public safety anti-nepotism rules against *constitutional* attacks, employees may have a source of protection in *statute*. The Washington discrimination law which prohibits marital discrimination has been interpreted to prohibit anti-nepotism rules *except* where the employer can establish a bona fide occupational qualification ("BFOQ") as a basis to enforce anti-nepotism standards. Employers have historically applied anti-nepotism rules where

    (1)   there is a documented conflict of interest;

    (2)   to avoid the appearance of improper influence;

    (3)   to protect confidentiality. The current status of restrictions on anti-nepotism rules under this statute is unclear because the statute has been amended to change the definition of marital

discrimination in a way that may adversely affect prior case law.

There is a statutory, but not a constitutional, right to choose one's own residence. In *McCarthy v. Philadelphia Civil Service Commission*, the United States Supreme Court ruled that there is *no constitutional prohibition* on municipal residence requirements, but there is a Washington state *statutory* prohibition. Under Washington law, the municipal civil service commission that regulates police and fire departments are prohibited from establishing such residency requirements; however, this restriction does not apply to sheriff's departments or

> **COURT DECISIONS CONCERNING THE RIGHT OF EMPLOYEES TO ASSOCIATE HAVE BEEN GIVEN A HIGH DEGREE OF PROTECTION TO PUBLIC SAFETY EMPLOYEES' RIGHT TO MAINTAIN PRIVATE RELATIONS, BUT HAVE ALLOWED RESTRICTIONS WHEN THOSE RELATIONS HAVE A DEMONSTRATIVE, NEGATIVE IMPACT ON THE WORKPLACE.**

fire districts. It should also be noted that the ban on residency rules does not keep an employer from adopting "distance mandates; the civil service law prohibition is one that keeps the agency from making the employee reside within the city's boundaries. (As to those agencies in which the Civil service law does not prohibit or regulate residency mandates, of where the mandate does not reach far enough, there nonetheless remains a *very clear* duty under PERC law to bargain such rules.)

Law enforcement departments commonly establish rules that prohibit employees from having contact with "known" criminals in a social setting. In the past, these regulations have almost been uniformly upheld, but there have been some recent challenges to these rules. Increasingly, the courts are giving these rules more and more scrutiny to make sure they are not vague or overbroad. One aspect is clear — such rules *cannot* interfere with family relationships so exceptions must be written into the rules for those relationships.

5. Privacy Rights in Off-Duty Conduct

Public safety departments frequently issue rules attempting to regulate off-duty conduct. Although arbitrators will closely scrutinize these rules as applied, and determine that they are "rational" and not "arbitrary or capricious," there is no *general* constitutional right violated by these rules. Therefore, though vague, rules such as "conduct unbecoming an officer" are held to be within an agencies legitimate sphere of enforcement. But the application of these rules is subject to court review. The general approach is to scrutinize the application of the rule using the test of whether the officers knew or should have known that such conduct would violate department norms.

One rule of thumb seems to be "when off-duty and out of uniform [an officer] can do privately what he wishes to do until such time as it materially and substantially impairs his usefulness as a [public officer]." Departments certainly retain the right to discipline and regulate for all criminal activity, including criminal sexual conduct such as acts of prostitution. In short, sex that is age inappropriate, paid-for, or involving an inherent conflict with one's job duties is not offered any protection. Regulation otherwise of consensual intimate activity is likely unconstitutional.

C. The Right to be Free of Unlawful Discrimination

The U.S. Constitution and state and federal laws prohibit various forms of discrimination. These laws and constitutional provisions, in various forms, prohibit discrimination based on race, color, national origin, gender, sexual orientation, age, disability and veteran's status. Disability discrimination is covered separately above, and in this section we focus on the three other discrimination laws subject to the greatest level of litigation: Race, Gender and Religion.

1. **Racial Discrimination**

Racial discrimination claims may be based on either direct and intentional discrimination or "adverse impact" discrimination. "Adverse impact" does not require proof of the employer's specific intent but only that the employment practice had an adverse statistical impact on protected groups.

When an adverse impact is shown, the burden will be on the employer to show that there is a business reason for a particular practice. The practical result of these rules is that employers are obligated to scrutinize closely and validate their own minimum qualification requirements.

Today, there is significant controversy surrounding the issue of affirmative action. There is also abundant misunderstanding about the scope of the current law: current law does not allow generalized preferential treatment without cause. Affirmative action programs can only be lawfully implemented to address some prior discrimination which has occurred in the workplace. These points seem to get lost on both sides of what has become a political debate.

2. **Gender Discrimination**

The same prohibitions on intentional and "disparate impact" discrimination applies to gender, as well. Hiring practices which involve size and physical strength requirements will be closely scrutinized. Sexual harassment is a form of gender discrimination and is prohibited by gender discrimination laws.

Sexual harassment usually arises in one of two forms:

(1) "quid pro quo" harassment or

(2) hostile work environment harassment. "Quid pro quo" harassment involves the conditioning of employment opportunities and benefits for the receipt of sexual favors. Consent is not a defense. The rules concerning "quid pro quo" sexual harassment are fairly clear.

The rules concerning hostile work environment sexual harassment are less clear. The general concept is that the conduct at issue must be "severe and pervasive" in order to establish a hostile work environment. Many courts have demonstrated a fairly high tolerance level for crude behavior so the concept that the conduct be both severe *and* pervasive need to underscored.

3. Religious Discrimination

Religious discrimination issues occasionally arise. Employers are required to "reasonably accommodate" religious faiths. This duty to accommodate does not extend to the point where accommodation creates an "undue hardship" in the workplace. A classic example of undue hardship is a scheduling conflict. If an accommodation of the schedule directly contradicts the parties CBA, it would be considered an "undue hardship" and the religious accommodation need not be made.

VI. The FLSA — The Right to be Paid for All Hours Worked

The right to be paid for wages, including overtime, is controlled both by the labor contract and the Fair Labor Standards Act (FLSA). Both the CBA and the FLSA establish *a floor*. Labor agreements can and often do exceed FLSA minimums. But when they do not, the FLSA still controls. *A labor organization may not waive its members' rights to wages under the FLSA.*

Overtime Threshold. Employees are entitled to payment for all "hours worked." Employees are entitled to pay at the overtime rate only when the "hours worked" exceed the applicable overtime threshold. Section 207(k) of the FLSA (sometimes referenced in shorthand form as "7k" permits public safety employers to adopt alternatives to the standard weekly 40 hour overtime threshold — for law enforcement and corrections officers, 171 hours in a 28 day period and for firefighters 212 hours in a 28 day period.

Employers may adopt "7k" periods shorter than 28 days, as well. But employees must act affirmatively to be covered by a "7k" exemption — otherwise the 7 day, 40 hour threshold applies. In other words, if the agency fails to assert a particular 7k cycle (and this is likely subject to a separate collective bargaining duty), and if FLSA litigation ensues, overtime will be measured on a 40 hour basis and a 7k cycle cannot be retroactively asserted.

Right to be Paid for Hours Worked. In general, the FLSA is designed to broadly protect employees. It does not matter whether or not the employer actually "ordered" you to do specific work. It is enough that they had actual or "constructive" knowledge that you were, in fact, doing the work. In terms of the FLSA such knowledge means that, under the law, they "suffered or permitted" the work and, therefore, must pay for it. Employers cannot turn a blind eye to work they know — or should know — is being performed.

The concept of the type of "work" that must be compensated is *broad* under the FLSA. *Almost any activity on behalf of the employer is likely "work."* The following are examples of the type of work of public safety employees that have been found to be frequently at issue in FLSA lawsuits and whether the work is compensable (must be paid) or not compensable:

- Pre-shift preparatory work, including the preparation of equipment and attendance at pre-shift briefings is compensable.

- Post-shift work, including finishing reports or putting away equipment, is compensable.

- "On call" time is generally *not* compensable when only a general readiness is required (so that the obligation to respond is fulfilled by maintaining contact through pagers or other electronic communication devices), but it may be compensable where the reporting limitations on the employee's time are severe.

- Meals and breaks are generally compensable where employees maintain their call responder status — it becomes non-compensable only where they are completely relieved of duty.

- Training time is generally compensable unless it relates to general education rather than job-specific classes.

- Off-duty work which is significant, such as care of a canine or vehicle maintenance, is compensable – but minor duties such as cleaning of a weapon or uniforms are likely noncompensable as "de minimis" activities.

The FLSA includes a number of pay requirements and the list is only a sample of the most frequent issues. If the employer has violated these requirements they have probably violated others and a complete audit of their pay practices may be in order.

Regular Rate. One of the most frequent FLSA violations is to fail to pay overtime based on the "regular rate" pay. Overtime must be at the rate of time and one half not only the base rate, but the regular rate. The regular rate must incorporate virtually all your pays and special premiums.

Compensatory Time. A frequent area of confusion concerning the FLSA is compensatory time. When an employee has accrued compensatory, the employee has the right to use that time except when it would cause an "undue hardship" upon the employer. According to a Department of Labor (DOL) interpretation, it is generally not an "undue hardship" for an employer to have to pay overtime to replace an individual seeking to use their earned compensatory time. This DOL interpretation has been controversial, though, and some courts, including the Ninth Circuit have declined to follow it.

Damages and Attorneys' Fees. The FLSA enforcement scheme contains built-in incentives for private enforcement of the statute. Prevailing parties are entitled to attorney fees and costs. And there is a presumption that plaintiffs are entitled to "liquidated" (double) damages. Employees with viable claims must not sleep on their rights. The statute of limitations is generally only two years and every day which passes results in the loss of another day of unpaid wages.

Conclusion

Yes, you do have legal rights. Just as the criminal suspects we discussed at the outset have a right to be advised of their *Miranda* rights, public safety employees need to be advised of their legal rights. Maybe what we need is a litany of those rights so employees can remember their right to be treated fairly. I hope that that the following serves as a useful summary of these rights:

1. You have a right to remain silent — except where you have been given a proper *Garrity* order.

2. You have a right to be represented — in discipline matters as well as in collective bargaining.

3. You have a right to present evidence on your behalf before you are disciplined and have a union representative assist in that presentation.

4. You have a right to be disciplined in a fair manner — using lawful investigation tactics and only where there is "just cause."

5. You have a right not to be unlawfully discriminated against — whether based on disability, pregnancy, gender, race or religion, or union activity.

6. You have a right to a reasonable accommodation of your medical conditions and not to be subject to intrusive and unreasonable medical and psychological examinations.

7. You have a right to be protected by the same United State Constitution which you have sworn to protect — including the right to speak on matters of public concern, the right

to be free of unreasonable searches and seizures, and the right to privacy and freedom in personal matters.

8. You have a right to be paid wages — for all of the hours you work.

YOU ARE ENTITLED TO THE PROTECTION OF THE UNITED STATES CONSTITUTION AND THE LAWS OF THIS LAND — NO LESS THAN THE CITIZENS THAT YOU SERVE AND PROTECT.

Made in the USA
San Bernardino, CA
31 January 2019